Contents

1 Match. Then write.

①  ②  ③  ④

ⓐ

ⓑ

ⓒ

ⓓ

___Hello___.
___I'm Rose___.

_____.
I'm Uncle Dan.

Hello.
_____ Charlie.

Hello. I'm
_____.

9 **Read and match.**
Then listen and check.

1 What's your name?
2 How old are you?
3 When's your birthday?
4 What's your favourite colour?
5 Do you like dogs?
6 What day is it today?
7 How are you?

a It's in August.
b I'm fine, thank you!
c My name's Rose.
d Blue.
e It's Tuesday.
f I'm eight.
g Yes, I do.

10 **Ask a friend and answer.**

1 What's your name?

2 What day is it today?

3 How are you today?

1 My toys

1 Follow and write.

| ~~ball~~ | bike | boat | car | doll | kite | lorry | teddy bear | train |

1

2

3

4

5

6

7

8

9

a It's a _____ .

b It's a _____ .

c It's a *ball* .

d It's a _____ .

e It's a _____ .

f It's a _____ .

g It's a _____ .

h It's a _____ .

i It's a _____ .

 **Look. Then read and circle.**

1 ((What's) / What are) this?

It's a (ball / (doll) / teddy bear).

2 (What's / What are) that?

It's a (boat / bike / train).

3 (What's / What are) these?

They're (kite / kites / lorries).

4 (What's / What are) those?

They're (bikes / bike / ball).

  Listen and write. Then draw and colour.

1

It's a ___train___.

It's _____.

2

They're _____.

They're _____.

_____.

3

It's a _____.

It's _____.

4 📖 ✏️ **Look and match.**

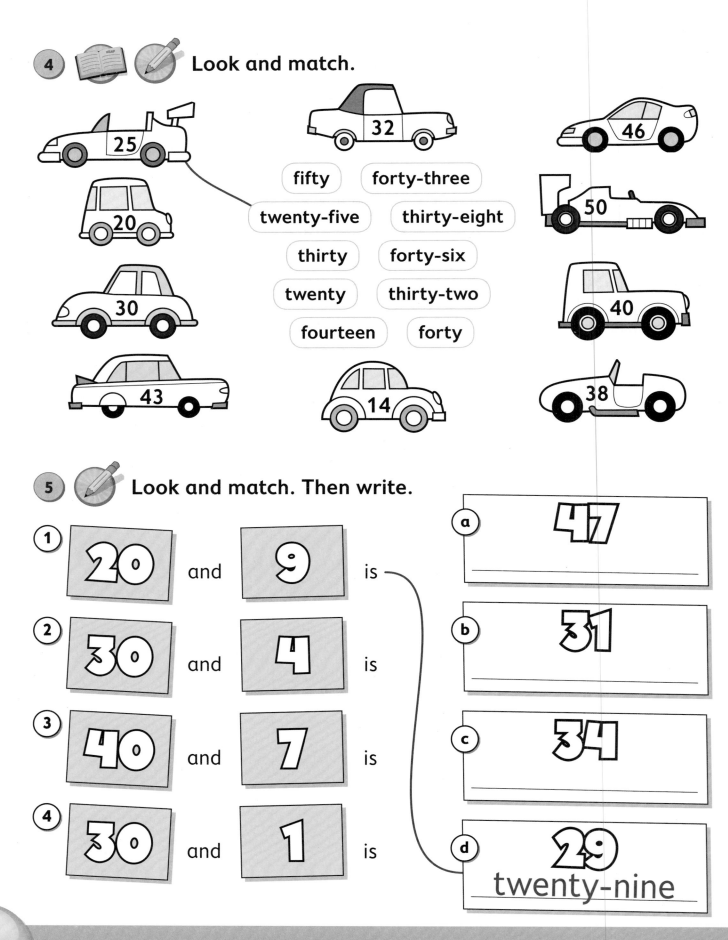

25   32   46

fifty   forty-three

twenty-five   thirty-eight

thirty   forty-six

twenty   thirty-two

fourteen   forty

20   50   40

30   40   38

43   14

5 ✏️ **Look and match. Then write.**

1 **20** and **9** is

2 **30** and **4** is

3 **40** and **7** is

4 **30** and **1** is

a **47**

b **31**

c **34**

d **29**
   twenty-nine

6 **Look and count. Then write.**

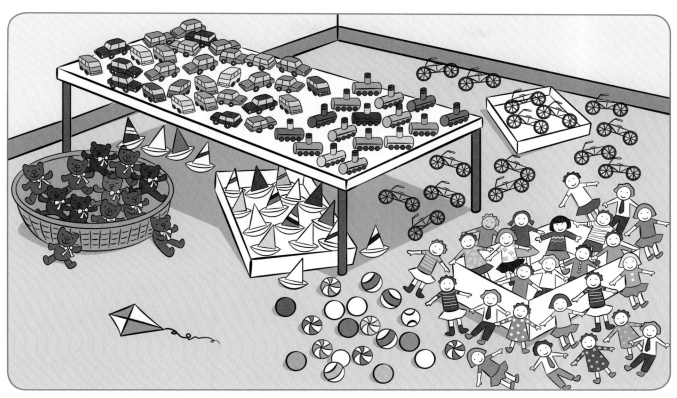

1 How many _____ **bikes** _____ are there?

There are _____ **fifteen bikes** _____.

2 _____ are there?

There are _____.

3 _____ are there?

There are _____.

4 _____ are there?

There is _____.

7   **Look and number. Then tell the story again.**

1

8   **Look and ✔. Then write about you.**

1

Good friends play together and share toys.

2

Good friends listen and help.

Think of a good friend.

_____ is a good friend.

What do you like?

We like _____

and _____.

1

9  **Read the words and circle.**

~~fish~~   rich   shell   ship

10 1:31 **Listen and link the letters.**

ch   c   h   sh

START   p   f   b   **FINISH**

s   sh   ch   s

11 1:32 **Listen and write the words.**

1 ch i n   2 ___ ___ ___

3 ___ ___ ___   4 ___ ___ ___

12   1:33 **Read aloud. Then listen and check.**

I can see a fish. I can see a shell.

13   **Look and write. Then find and draw the missing word.**

bike   boat   bus   car   ~~helicopter~~   lorry   plane   train

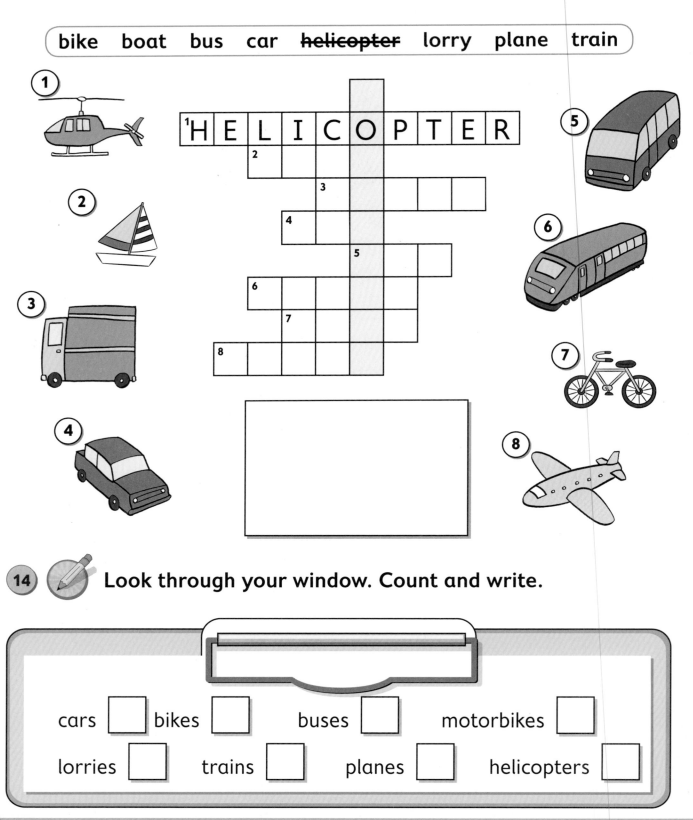

1 H E L I C O P T E R

14 **Look through your window. Count and write.**

cars ☐ bikes ☐ buses ☐ motorbikes ☐

lorries ☐ trains ☐ planes ☐ helicopters ☐

15 **Complete the picture and match.**

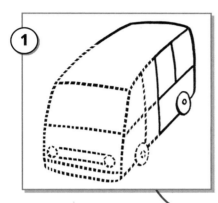

1

2

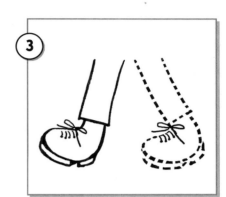

3

a I walk to school.

b I go to school by bus.

c I go to school by car.

16   **Read and write. How do you travel?**

| by bike | by boat | by bus | by car |
| by helicopter | by lorry | by plane | by train |

1 I go to the library _____ .

2 I go to the shop _____ .

3 I go to the park _____ .

4 I go to school _____ .

17   **Read and circle. Then colour.**

It's a ((car) / boat).
It's blue.

It's a (bike / train).
It's yellow.

It's a (doll / teddy bear).
It's purple.

18 **Look and circle. Then write.**

1

(What's this?) / What are those?

It's a _____ boat _____ .

2

What's this? / What are these?

They're _____ .

3

What's that? / What are these?

_____

4

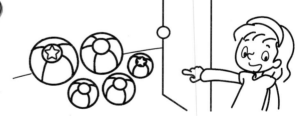

What's that? / What are those?

_____

19 **Look at Activity 18. Count and write.**

1 How many cars are there? There are _____ cars.

2 How many balls are there? _____

20  **Read and write. Then colour.**

bike ~~favourite~~ school teddy bear

These are my
¹ __favourite__ toys.

This is my favourite
² _____ bear. His
name's Fred and he's brown.

And this is my ³_____.
It's red and black. I go to
⁴_____ by bike.

21   **Draw your favourite toys. Then write.**

These are my favourite toys.

_____

_____

_____

_____

_____

2 My family

1 Look and write.

> aunt ~~cousin~~ daughter
> grandad granny son uncle

This is my dad.

This is my mum.

This is my brother.

1 This is my __cousin__.

2 This is my _____.

3 This is my _____.

4 This is my _____.

5 This is my _____.

6 This is my _____.

7 This is my _____.

Look, circle and write.

~~aunt~~ cousin daughter son

1 Who's (he / (she))?

(He's / (She's)) my
aunt_____.

2 Who's (he / she)?

(He's / She's) my
_____.

3 Who's (he / she)?

(He's / She's) my
_____.

4 (He's / She's) my
_____.

 **Look, read and write.**

attic~~attic~~ bedroom   flat   hall   kitchen   living room

Where's my granny?

She's in the _____ **attic** _____.

Where's my uncle?

He's in the _____.

Where's my aunt?

_____ in the _____.

Where's my daughter?

_____ in the _____.

Where's my son?

_____ in the _____.

Where's my cousin?

_____ in the _____.

4  **Read and colour.**

1 The red car is on the bed.

2 The purple car is behind the backpack.

3 The blue car is under the chair.

4 The yellow car is on the desk. It's next to the lamp.

5 The green car is in the backpack.

5 **Look at the picture again. Write *True* or *False*.**

1 There are two beds. _____ True _____

2 There are three desks. _____

3 There are six cars. _____

4 There's a lamp on the desk. _____

6   **Read and circle. Then match.**

1 Where's Charlie's grandad?
He's in the (flat / shop).

2 Where's Charlie's mum?
She's in the (garden / bathroom).

3 Where's Charlie's uncle?
He's in the (shop / kitchen).

4 Where's Charlie's aunt?
She's in the (attic / library).

7 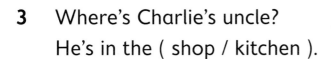 **Read and write.**
Then draw your family.

How many aunts have you got?

I've got _____.

How many uncles have you got?

_____

How many cousins have you got?

_____

8  **Read the words and circle.**

| ~~bath~~ | thick | thin | this |

9  **Listen and link the letters.**

s   th   th   sh

START   a   r   s   FINISH

th   z   ch   th

10 **Listen and write the words.**

1 th   i   s

2 ___ ___ ___

3 ___ ___ ___

4 ___ ___ ___

11 **Read aloud. Then listen and check.**

This is a thick book. That is a thin book.

12   **Listen and number. Then write.**

| baby   children   grandparents   ~~parents~~ |

a

_____

b

_____

c

1

parents

d

_____

13 **Read and match.**

①    ②    ③    ④

They're young.   She's young.   They're old.   He's young.

14 Look and write.   garden   house   treehouse

1

This is a

_____.

2

This is a

_____.

3

This is a

_____.

15  A treehouse home! Listen and number.

   Read and write. Then match.

1 Where's my daughter?

___She's___ in the garden.

2 Where's your aunt?

_____ in the house.

3 _____ my cousin?

He's in the flat.

  **Read and draw.**

My teddy bear is in the bathroom.

My ball is on the bed.

My kite is next to the ball.

My doll is under the bed.

2

18  **Read and write.**

~~aunt~~   garden   one   these   two

This is my uncle and
¹ __aunt__ and
² _____ are my cousins.

They are in my ³ _____.

I've got ⁴ _____
cousins. They are babies.

They're ⁵ _____
year old.

19 **Draw some of your family. Then write.**

This is my _____

and _____.

_____

_____

_____

_____

_____

3 Move your body

1 Look and write.

clap   move   nod   point   ~~shake~~   stamp   touch   wave

 **1**

 **2**

 **3**

<u>Shake</u> your body.   _____ your arms.   _____ your head.

 4

 5

_____ your toes.   _____ your feet.

 6

7

8

_____ your fingers.   _____ your hands.   _____ your legs.

Read and circle.

1

(He / (She)) can shake
(his / (her)) body.

2

I (can / can't) touch
(my / your) toes.

3

(He / She) can stamp
(his / her) feet.

4

I (can / can't) wave
(my / your) arms.

3   **Listen and number.**

a

b

c

d 1

4 Look and match. Then write the missing letters.

1

2

3

4

5

6

7

8

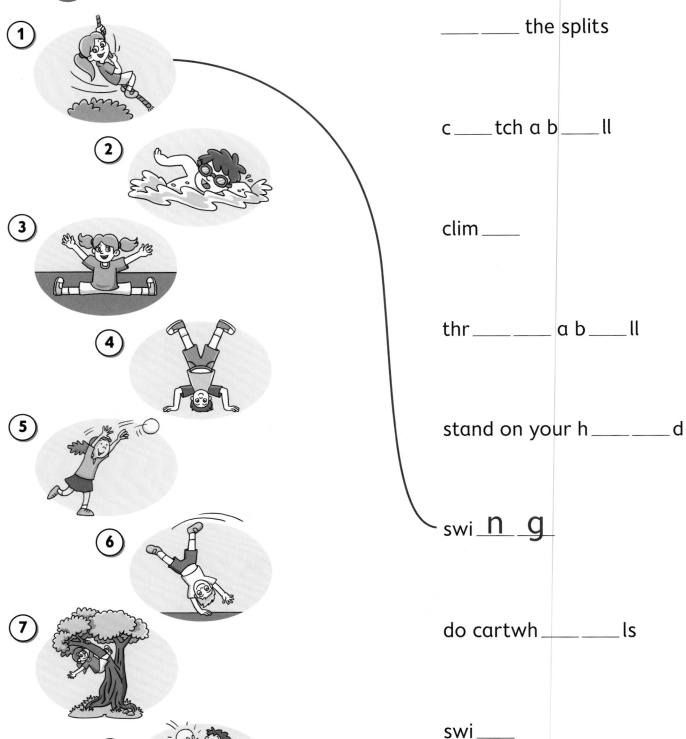

_____ _____ the splits

c_____tch a b_____ll

clim_____

thr_____ _____ a b_____ll

stand on your h_____ _____d

swi_n_ _g_

do cartwh_____ _____ls

swi_____

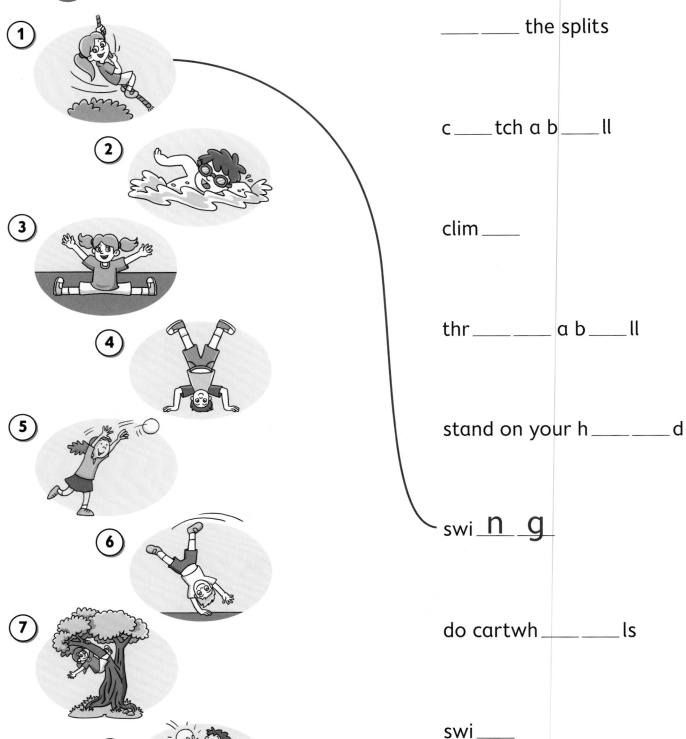

5 Look, write and circle.

climb   do cartwheels   ~~do the splits~~   swim

1
Can he ___do the splits___?

(Yes, he can.) / No, he can't.

2
Can you _____?

Yes, I can. / No, I can't.

3
Can he _____?

Yes, he can. / No, he can't.

4
Can you _____?

Yes, I can. / No, I can't.

6   **Read and match.**

1  Jump! Touch your toes!

2  This is fun!

3 Er, can you help? It's the bus.

4 You can push fast!

 **a**

 **b**

 **c**

 **d**

7 **Write ✓ = exercise or ✗ = not exercise.**

 **1**

 **2**

 **3**

 **4**

 **5**

 **6**

 **7**

 **8**

8   **Read the words and circle.**

ink   ~~ring~~   sing   sink

9 **Listen and link the letters.**

g   nk   ng   c

START   n   sh   th   FINISH

ng   k   m   nk

10 **Listen and write the words.**

1   p   i   ng   2   ___ ___ ___

3   ___ ___ ___   4   ___ ___ ___

11 **Read aloud. Then listen and check.**

Dad can sing. The girl can sing.

12 **Look and write.**

hop

~~hop~~
pull
push
skip

_____

_____

13   **Read and find. Then number.**

☐ Wave your arms.

☐ Jump.

☐ Clap your hands.

☐ Touch your toes.

☐ Skip.

1 Hop.

14   **Look and match.**

 **1**

 **2**

 **3**

 **4**

a tug of war

b sack race

c egg-and-spoon race

d three-legged race

15   **Read and write about yourself.**

Yes, I can.   No, I can't.

1 Can you run fast? _____

2 Can you kick a ball? _____

3 Can you touch your toes? _____

4 Can you point your toes? _____

5 Can you throw a ball? _____

Look and write.

| ~~climb~~ | do the splits | hop | skip | swim | swing |

1

Can she __climb__ ?

Yes, she can.

2

Can he _____ ?

_____ , he can't.

3

Can he _____ ?

Yes, _____ .

4

Can _____ ?

_____ .

5

_____ ?

_____ .

6

_____ ?

_____ .

17 **What can you do? Read and circle.**

1 I (can / can't) do cartwheels.

2 I (can / can't) swim.

3 I (can / can't) stand on my head.

4 I (can / can't) hop.

5 I (can / can't) do the splits.

6 I (can / can't) run fast.

7 I (can / can't) catch a ball.

8 I (can / can't) climb trees.

18 Look and read. Then write *can* or *can't*.

I ¹ ___can___ shake my body and
I ² _____ skip.
I ³ _____ catch a
ball and I ⁴ _____
do cartwheels.
I ⁵ _____ hop.
And I ⁶ _____
touch my toes!

19 Look and ✔ or ✗. Then write about yourself or a friend.

I can _____
and I _____.

_____

_____

_____

_____

ABOUT ME

4 My face

1 Look and write.

ears eyes ~~face~~ hair mouth nose

1 ___face___

2 _____

3 _____

4 _____

5 _____

6 _____

2 📖 ✏️ **Read. Then look and write 1 or 2.**

① [face 1]

② [face 2]

a I've got big eyes. [2]

b I've got short hair. [ ]

c I haven't got a big mouth. [ ]

d I've got long hair. [ ]

e I've got small eyes. [ ]

f I haven't got a big nose. [ ]

3 📖 ✏️ **Look, read and circle.**

1 Have you got small ears?

(Yes, I have.) / No, I haven't.

2 Have you got long hair?

Yes, I have. / No, I haven't.

3 Has she got big eyes?

Yes, she has. / No, she hasn't.

4 Has he got a small nose?

Yes, he has. / No, he hasn't.

   **4** Read and circle.

1

She's got
((long) / short)
hair.

2

She's got
(neat / messy)
hair.

3

He's got
(long / short)
hair.

4

She's got
(neat / messy)
hair.

5

He's got
(blond / dark)
hair.

6

He's got
(straight / curly)
hair.

5   **Listen and ✔. Then draw.**

✔ big eyes

☐ big nose

☐ short, curly hair

☐ small eyes

☐ small nose

☐ long, straight hair

6 **2:13** **Listen and circle. Then look and write.**

Granny

Ruth

Max

Uncle Ed

1 (straight) / curly / (messy) / blond   It's ___Ruth___.

2 messy / neat / blond / red   It's _____.

3 long / short / straight / curly   It's _____.

4 messy / neat / curly / dark   It's _____.

7 **Look at Activity 6 and write.**

1 Granny has got ___short, curly hair___.
   Her hair is ___short and curly___.

2 Ruth has got _____, _____ hair.
   Her hair is _____ and _____.

3 Max has got _____, _____ hair.
   His hair is _____ and _____.

4 Uncle Ed has got _____, _____ hair.
   His hair is _____ and _____.

5 I've got _____, _____ hair.
   My hair is _____ and _____.

8   **Look and write.**

1 Has she got a _**small**_ nose?

Yes, she _____.

2 _____ got black hair.

He _____ got blond hair.

3 Her _____ is long.

4 _____ hair is messy.

| hair |
| has |
| hasn't |
| He's |
| His |
| ~~small~~ |

9   2:15 **Listen and number.**

 a

 b

 1

10   **Read the words and circle.**

~~snail~~   rain   tail   feet

11 **Listen and link the letters.**

2:19

ai   e   a   o

START   ee   ai   ee   **FINISH**

a   u   i   ai

12 **Listen and write the words.**

2:20

1 _s_ _ee_ ___   2 ___ ___ ___

3 ___ ___ ___   4 ___ ___ ___

13 **Read aloud. Then listen and check.**

2:21

The cat has got a tail. The cat has got four feet.

14 **Count and write.**

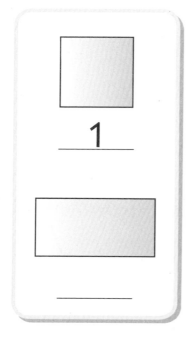

1

_____

_____

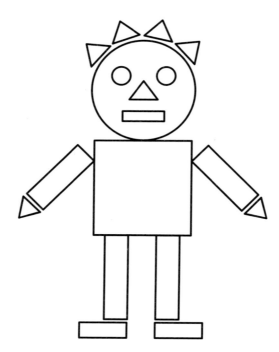

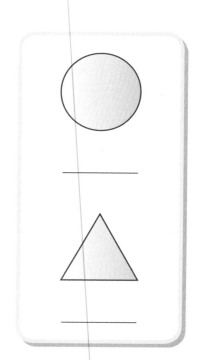

_____

_____

15  **Listen, look at Activity 14 and circle.**

1 (Yes) / No   **2** Yes / No   **3** Yes / No   **4** Yes / No

16 **Draw. Use the shapes in Activity 14. Then write.**

It's a _____.

17  **Read and circle.**

1

It's a (painting / mask).

It's got (big / small) eyes.

2

It's a (mosaic / statue).

It's got (long / short) hair.

18   **Look at the mosaic pictures. Colour and write.**

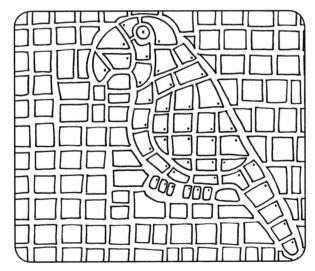

What's this?

It's a _____.

What's this?

_____

19   **Read and write.**

1 Has she got big eyes?

<u>Yes, she has</u>.

2 Has she got dark hair?

_____.

3 Has she got small ears?

_____.

4 Has she got a big nose?

_____.

20   **Draw. Then read and write.**

1 He's got short, blond hair. It's curly. Who is it? It's <u>Nick</u>.

2 She's got long, blond hair. It's straight and messy.

Who is it? _____

3 She's got long, blond hair. It's curly and neat.

Who is it? _____

  **Read and circle.**

me   George

This is me and my best friend. ¹(**His** / Her) name's George.

My hair is short and ²(dark / blond). I've got ³(big / small) eyes. My eyes are brown. I've got a ⁴(big / small) mouth and ⁵(big / small) ears!

George's hair is ⁶(long / short) and ⁷(dark / blond). His hair is ⁸(neat / messy). He's got ⁹(big / small) eyes and a ¹⁰(big / small) mouth.

   Draw yourself and a friend and write.

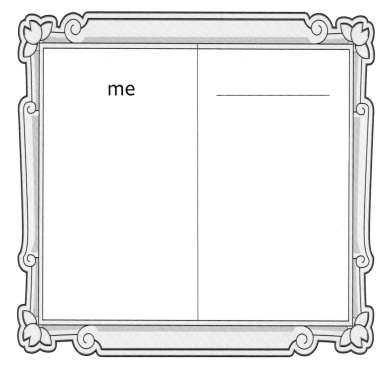

me   _____

This is me and my best friend.

_____

_____

_____

_____

_____

5 Animals

1 Look and write.

cow   duck   ~~goat~~   hen   horse   sheep   turkey

1 __goat__
2 _____
3 _____
4 _____
5 _____
6 _____
7 _____

 **Listen and number.**

a

b

c

d  1

3 **Look at Activity 2. Read, write and colour.**

1 What are these? They've got big bodies and black feet.
They're white. They've got black faces. They're _sheep_.

2 What's this? It's got a big mouth and two big feet. It's yellow.
It's a _____.

3 What's this? It's got four legs. It's brown.
It's a _____.

4 What are these? They're big and black. They've got long legs.
They're _____.

Look and write.

bat ~~bat~~ crow fox frog lizard owl rat skunk

1 _bat_

2 _____

3 _____

4 _____

5 _____

6 _____

7 _____

8 _____

  Read, match and write.

1 It's got a long tail.
It's brown.

a

They're _____.

2 They're small and green.
They've got big eyes.

b

It's a _fox_.

3 They're thin and black.
They've got two legs.

c

They're _____.

6  **Read and circle the mistakes. Then write.**

1

It's a frog. It's (big.)

It isn't ___big___ . It's ___small___ .

2

They're goats. They're very thin.

They aren't _____ .

They're _____ .

3

It's a duck. It's big.

It isn't a _____ .

It's a _____ .

4

They're skunks. They're green.

They aren't _____ .

They're _____ and _____ .

7   **Look at Activity 6 and write the answers.**

> Yes, it is.   ~~No, it isn't.~~   Yes, they are.   No, they aren't.

1 Is the hen small? _____ No, it isn't. _____

2 Are the foxes thin? _____

3 Is the frog small? _____

4 Are the skunks red? _____

8 **Read and draw.**

STORY

What's that?

1 It's a cow.
2 It's a goat.
3 They're hens.
4 It's a skunk.

9 **Look and match.**

VALUES

1

2

3

4

a

b

c

MILK

d

10  **Read the words and circle.**

~~boat~~   goat   light   soap

11 2:45 **Listen and link the letters.**

a   igh   o   a

START —   oa   **FINISH**

        i

        oa   ch   i   igh

12 2:46 **Listen and write the words.**

1 __s__ __igh__   2 ___ ___

3 ___ ___   4 ___ ___

13 2:47 **Read aloud. Then listen and check.**

The goat has got some soap. The goat has got a boat.

14  **Look and read. Then write and circle.**

1  I'm a _____ **fox** _____.
I'm ((asleep) / awake) in the day.

bat
cow
duck
~~fox~~
owl

2  I'm a _____.
I'm (asleep / awake) at night.

3 I'm an _____.
I'm (asleep / awake) at night.

4  I'm a _____.
I'm (asleep / awake) in the day.

5  I'm a _____.
I'm (asleep / awake) in the day.

15  **Draw the animals from Activity 14.**

1
day

2
night

16 **Look and match.**

1 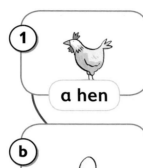 a hen

2  an ostrich

a 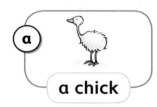 a chick

b  an egg

c 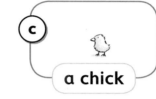 a chick

d 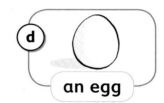 an egg

17  **Read and write _True_ or _False_.**

1   Ostriches are birds.   <u>True</u>

2   They aren't big. They're small.   _____

3   They've got two legs.   _____

4   They've got very short legs.   _____

5   They can't fly.   _____

6   The father ostrich is brown.   _____

7   Ostrich eggs aren't small. They're big. _____

18  **Correct the false sentences.**

<u>Ostriches are big.</u>

_____

19   **Listen, ✓ and colour.**

1 **a** 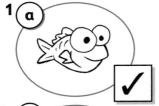 ✓ **b**  ☐

2 **a**  ☐ **b**  ☐

3 **a**  ☐ **b**  ☐

4 **a**  ☐ **b**  ☐

20  **Look, read and write.**

1 Is the cow big?

  Yes, it is.

2 Are the sheep white?

  _____

3 Is it a hen?

  _____

  It's an _____.

4 Are they foxes?

  _____

  They're _____.

21  **Read and write.**

asleep   awake   big   fox   four   horse   tail   ~~white~~

My favourite animal is very big and
1_____**white**_____.

It's got 2_____ legs and a
long 3_____.

It's got a 4_____ nose.

It's 5_____ in the day.

It's 6_____ at night.

Is it a 7_____?

No, it isn't. It's a 8_____!

22 **Draw your favourite animal. Then circle and write.**

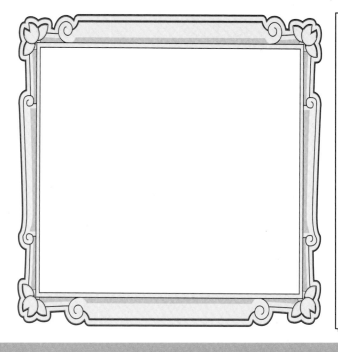

My favourite animal is (big / small)
and _____.

It's got _____

_____

_____

_____

6 Food

1 Look and write. Then draw.

1 _eggs_ ✓

2 _____ ✗

3 _____ ✗

4 _____ ✗

5 _____ ✓

6 _____ ✓

7 _____ ✓

8 _____ ✗

9 _____ ✗

apples
bananas
burgers
chicken
~~eggs~~

fish
pizza
rice
salad

2 **Look and write.**

| apples   bananas   ~~chicken~~   eggs |

1

I like ___chicken___.

2

I don't like _____.

3

She likes _____.

4

He doesn't like _____.

3 **Look at Activity 2. Read and match.**

1 Does Charlie like apples?

2 Does Rose like chicken?

3 Does Ola like bananas?

4 Does Uncle Dan like eggs?

a Yes, she does.

b No, he doesn't.

c Yes, she does.

d No, he doesn't.

4   **Read and answer.**

1 Do you like burgers? _____

2 Do you like salad? _____

5  **Look and match.**

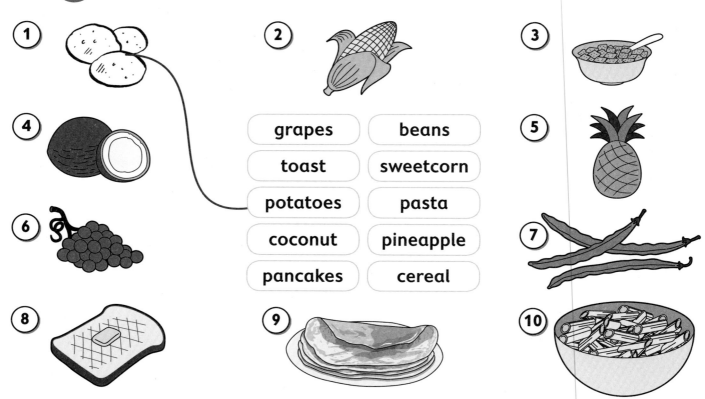

① ②

③ ④ ⑤

grapes | beans
toast | sweetcorn
potatoes | pasta
coconut | pineapple
pancakes | cereal

⑥ ⑦

⑧ ⑨ ⑩

6 **Look and write. Then read and number.**

~~breakfast~~ dinner lunch

① breakfast

②

③

ⓐ I like chicken and apples. ☐

ⓑ I like toast and eggs. 1

ⓒ I like fish and vegetables. I don't like rice. ☐

7 Look and write.

cereal

grapes

fish

beans

There's some...

rice

There are some...

burgers

rice

potatoes

chicken

8  Look at Activity 7. Read and write the answers.

~~Yes, there is.~~   No, there isn't.   Yes, there are.   No, there aren't.

1 Is there any rice? _____ Yes, there is.

2 Is there any pizza? _____

3 Are there any bananas? _____

4 Are there any burgers? _____

Lesson 4

61

9 📖 ✏️ **Read and ✔.**

		YES	NO
1	Charlie likes apple juice.	✔	
2	Rose doesn't like apples.		
3	Uncle Dan likes pineapple for lunch.		
4	Ola likes banana milkshakes.		
5	Charlie's favourite cake is chocolate cake.		
6	Uncle Dan likes chicken and rice for dinner.		
7	Rose likes milk.		
8	Charlie likes salad for dinner.		

10 ✏️ **Look and circle the healthy food and snacks.**

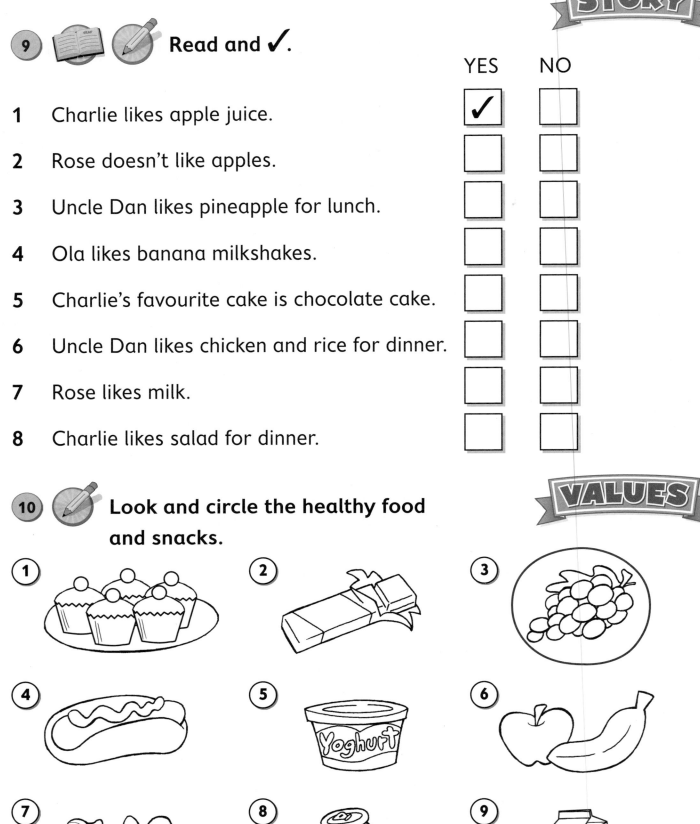

11  **Read the words and circle.**

~~book~~   foot   look   moon

12 🎧 **2:67** **Listen and link the letters.**

ee   igh   e   oa

START — a   oo   o   **FINISH**

oo   ai   ai   oo

13 🎧 **2:68** **Listen and write the words.**

1 __t__ __oo__   2 _____ _____

3 _____ _____   4 _____ _____

14 🎧 **2:69** **Read aloud. Then listen and check.**

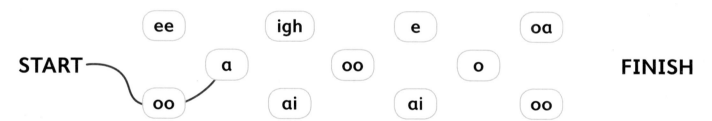

Look at the big moon. Look at the book, too.

15 Look and write.

cook   ~~cut~~
fry   mix

 1

 2

 3

 4

cut _____   _____   _____   _____

16 Recipes. Read and write.

1

Hot fruit salad

a

Cut some fruit.

b

_____ the fruit
in a pan.

c

_____ the _____.

2

Pasta salad

a

_____ some pasta.

b

_____ some sweetcorn.

c

Mix the _____
and _____.

3

Fish and chips

a

_____ some _____.

b

_____ some potatoes.

c

_____ the potatoes.

Wider World

17 2:73 **Listen and circle.**

1 She likes (/  / )

for (breakfast / lunch / dinner).

2 He likes ( / /)

for (breakfast / lunch / dinner).

3 He likes (/ / )

for (breakfast / lunch / dinner).

18   **Complete the sentences and write about food in your country.**

	me	my friend
Do you like mushrooms for breakfast?		
Do you like pasta for lunch?		
Do you like fish and chips for dinner?		
Do you like _____?		
Do you like _____?		
Do you like _____?		

19 **Listen and circle. Then write.**

I like...
cereal
chicken
cheese
fish
apples
salad

I don't like...
toast
pizza
bread
bananas
eggs
rice

1 He ___likes chicken___

and _____.

2 He _____

or _____.

20 **Read and circle. Then draw.**

This is my breakfast.
There's (some / any) cereal and there's (some / any) toast.
There are (some / any) bananas and there's (some / any) juice.
There isn't (some / any) cheese and there aren't (some / any) apples.
I like breakfast!

21 **Read and write.**

| any | like | don't | fruit | ~~some~~ |

This is my favourite dinner.

There's ¹ __some__ pizza and there's some salad.

I ² _____ pizza and salad.

There aren't ³ _____ burgers. I ⁴ _____ like burgers.

And there's some fruit. I like ⁵ _____.

But I don't like bananas.

22   **Draw your favourite dinner and write.**

This is my favourite dinner.

_____

_____

_____

_____

_____

_____

_____

7 Clothes

 **Find and write. Then colour.**

| dress | hat | jacket | skirt | shoe | socks | ~~T-shirt~~ | trousers |

1 an orange   T-shirt

2 blue _____

3 a pink _____

4 a red _____

5 a brown _____

6 green _____

7 a purple _____

8 a black _____

2 ✏️✏️ **Read and colour. Then read and write.**

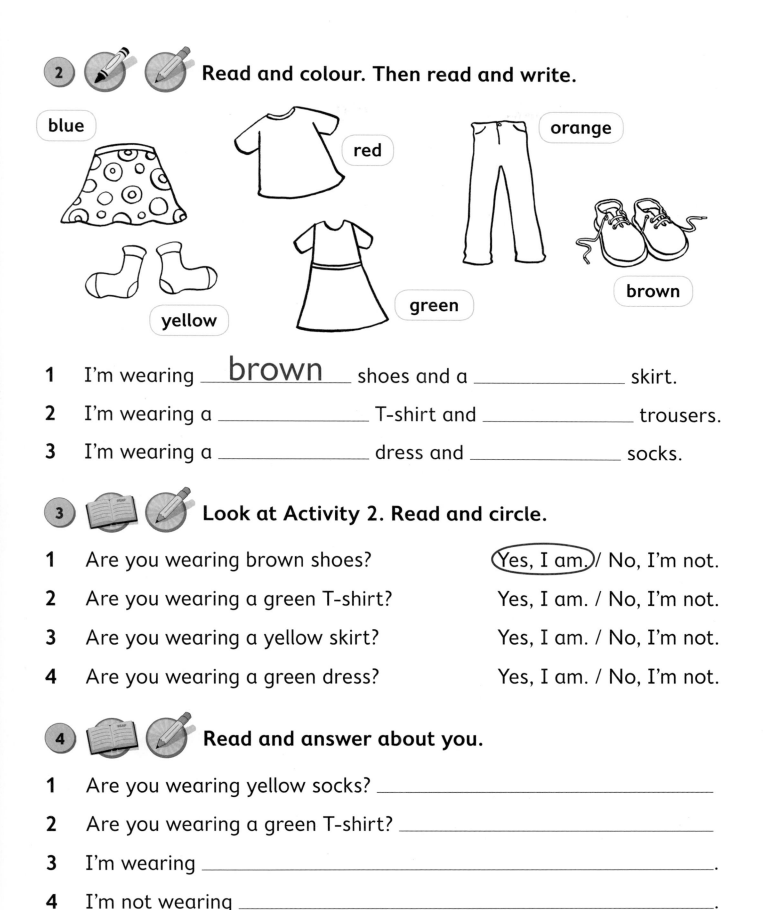

blue

red

orange

green

yellow

brown

1   I'm wearing ____brown____ shoes and a _____ skirt.

2   I'm wearing a _____ T-shirt and _____ trousers.

3   I'm wearing a _____ dress and _____ socks.

3 📖✏️ **Look at Activity 2. Read and circle.**

1   Are you wearing brown shoes?   (Yes, I am.)/ No, I'm not.

2   Are you wearing a green T-shirt?   Yes, I am. / No, I'm not.

3   Are you wearing a yellow skirt?   Yes, I am. / No, I'm not.

4   Are you wearing a green dress?   Yes, I am. / No, I'm not.

4 📖✏️ **Read and answer about you.**

1   Are you wearing yellow socks? _____

2   Are you wearing a green T-shirt? _____

3   I'm wearing _____.

4   I'm not wearing _____.

Look and write.

bed	boots	jumper	~~pyjamas~~	pyjamas	school	shoes	T-shirt

1

Take off your _pyjamas_.

2

Put on your _____.

3

Put on your _____.

4

It's time for _____.

5

Take off your _____.

6

Take off your _____.

7

Put on your _____.

8

It's time for _____.

6   **Listen and match. Then colour.**

7  **Look, read and circle. Then colour.**

①  Would you like a red jumper?
(Yes, I would.) / No, I wouldn't.
I'd like a ((red jumper) / red shirt).

②  Would you like white trainers?
Yes, I would. / No, I wouldn't.
I'd like (a pink boot / pink boots).

③  Would you like a yellow jacket?
Yes, I would. / No, I wouldn't.
I'd like a (yellow shirt / yellow skirt).

④  Would you like blue pyjamas?
Yes, I would. / No, I wouldn't.
I'd like (a blue pyjamas / blue pyjamas).

8   **Colour. Then write.**

1 I'm wearing a

_____

_____.

2 I'm wearing a

_____

_____.

9   **Look and write.**

~~Good morning.~~ Goodbye!   Good night. I'm sorry.   Please.   Thank you.

Good morning.

72 **Lesson 5**

ar ir
or ur

10   **Read the words and circle.**

~~car~~ girl shark surf

11 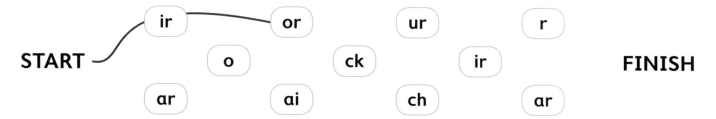 **Listen and link the letters.**

ir   or   ur   r

START   o   ck   ir   **FINISH**

ar   ai   ch   ar

12  **Listen and write the words.**

1   <u>s</u>   <u>ir</u>   2   _____ _____

3   _____ _____   4   _____ _____

13  **Read aloud. Then listen and check.**

See the girl surf. See the shark surf!

14 **Look and write.**

chef   firefighter   ~~nurse~~   police officer

1

2

3

4

She's a
__nurse__.

He's a
_____.

He's a
_____.

She's a
_____.

15  **Read. Then look at Activity 14 and number.**

a I'm wearing a shirt, a black skirt and black shoes. I'm wearing a hat. ☐

b I'm wearing a white dress, a hat and black shoes. I'm not wearing a helmet. [1]

c I'm wearing a coat and boots. I'm wearing a big helmet. ☐

d I'm wearing a T-shirt and trousers. I'm wearing white shoes and a tall hat. ☐

Wider World

16   **Colour and play.**

a

b

Are you wearing a yellow shirt?

Yes, I am.

No, I'm not.

17   **Look at Activity 16 and write.**

I'm wearing a _____ shirt and a _____ skirt. I'm wearing _____ boots. And I've got a _____ hat with flowers on it!

I'm wearing _____ trousers and a _____ jacket. I'm wearing _____ shoes. And I've got a _____ hat!

18 🎧 3:26 **Listen and ✓.**

1	purple dress ☐	pink dress ✓	pink skirt ☐
2	black trainers ☐	white trainers ☐	blue shoes ☐
3	purple skirt ☐	purple dress ☐	pink skirt ☐
4	brown shoes ☐	red socks ☐	red shoes ☐

19 📖 ✏️ **Read and number. Then colour.**

1 I'm wearing yellow pyjamas.

2 I'm wearing red shoes.

3 I'm wearing black boots.

4 I'm wearing a purple jumper.

a ☐

b ☐

c 1

d ☐

20 📖 ✏️ **What are you wearing? Read and circle.**

1 Are you wearing pink pyjamas?   Yes, I am. / No, I'm not.

2 Are you wearing white socks?   Yes, I am. / No, I'm not.

3 Are you wearing black shoes?   Yes, I am. / No, I'm not.

4 Are you wearing glasses?   Yes, I am. / No, I'm not.

I CAN DO IT!

 ABOUT ME

21  **Read and write. Then colour.**

| are | is | like | these | this | ~~wearing~~ |

I'm ¹ **wearing** my favourite clothes. ² _____ are my favourite jeans and ³ _____ is my favourite T-shirt. My jeans ⁴ _____ blue and my T-shirt ⁵ _____ red. I'm not wearing black trainers. I'm wearing white trainers. I'd ⁶ _____ some black trainers. I'm wearing a green cap.

22 **Draw your favourite clothes and write.**

I'm wearing my favourite clothes.

_____

_____

_____

_____

_____

8 Weather

1 Look and write.

cloudy   rainy   snowy   stormy   ~~sunny~~   windy

(1) What's the weather like?

It's ___sunny___.

(2)

It's _____.

(3)

It's _____.

(4) What's the weather like?

It's _____.

(5)

It's _____.

(6)

It's _____.

2   **Listen and write. Then draw.**

rainy ~~snowy~~ sunny windy

1 He likes ___snowy___ days.

2 She doesn't like _____ days.

3 She likes _____ days.

4 He doesn't like _____ days.

3  **Read, write and circle.**

1 What's the weather like today?   It's _____.

2 Do you like sunny days?   Yes, I do. / No, I don't.

3 Do you like cloudy days?   Yes, I do. / No, I don't.

4 Do you like stormy days?   Yes, I do. / No, I don't.

Look and write. | ride   take   fly   go   ~~make~~   read |

1 Let's __make__
a snowman.

2 Let's _____
for a walk.

3 Let's _____
a bike.

4 Let's _____
a photo.

5 Let's _____
a kite.

6 Let's _____
a book.

   Look, read and write.

Monday	Tuesday	Wednesday	Thursday	Friday	Saturday

1   It's snowy. What day is it today?   It's __Saturday__ .

2   It's windy. What day is it today?   It's _____ .

3   It's rainy. What day is it today?   It's _____ .

4   It's sunny. What day is it today?   It's _____ .

5   It's stormy. What day is it today?   It's _____ .

6   It's cloudy. What day is it today?   It's _____ .

6 **Look and circle.**

1. That hat is (**mine** / yours)!

2. This hat is (mine / yours)!

3. Those boots are (mine / yours)!

4. And these boots are (mine / yours)!

 7 **Follow and write _his_ or _hers_.**

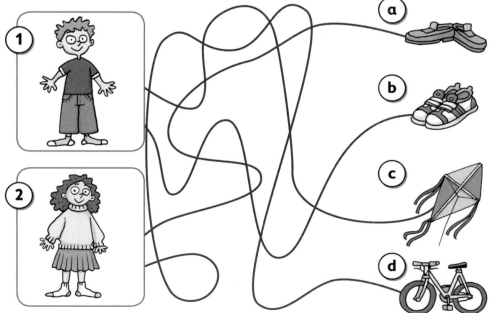

a. These shoes are _hers_.

b. These trainers are _____.

c. This kite is _____.

d. This bike is _____.

8 **Look and number. Then write.**

a

It's _____.

b `1`

It's _____ rainy _____.

c

It's _____.

d

It's _____.

9 **Look and ✔ the things you can share with other people.**

	friend(s)	sister(s)	brother(s)	parents

10   **Read the words and circle.**

~~boy~~ cow cowboy down

11 **Listen and link the letters.**

| ar | o | h | w |

START   j   oy   oy   **FINISH**

ow ——— y   p   ow

12 **Listen and write the words.**

1 OW l   2 ___ ___

3 ___ ___   4 ___ ___

13   **Read aloud. Then listen and check.**

The boy watches the cowboy. The cow watches the boy.

14  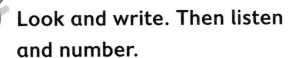 **Look and write. Then listen and number.**

~~cold~~   freezing   hot   warm

a

b

c

d

1

cold

15  **Read, look and ✓ or ✗.**

Monday	Tuesday	Wednesday	Thursday	Friday	Saturday	Sunday

1 It's Tuesday. It's windy. ✓   **2** It's Saturday. It's stormy. ☐

3 It's Thursday. It's rainy. ☐   **4** It's Sunday. It's cloudy. ☐

5 It's Monday. It's snowy. ☐   **6** It's Friday. It's sunny. ☐

16   **Listen and write.**

| ~~August~~ January July March September |

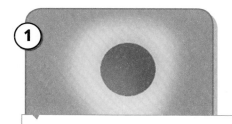

1

It's ___August___.
It's ___summer___. It's sunny.

2

It's _____.
It's _____. It's windy.

3

It's _____.
_____
_____ snowy.

4

_____
_____
_____

17  **What's your favourite weather? Read and write.**

My birthday is in _____.

The weather is _____.

My favourite month is _____.

The weather is _____.

18 **Read, look and write A or B.**

Picture A

Picture B

1 It's cloudy. A **2** I'm wearing a T-shirt and trousers. ☐

3 I've got a train. ☐ **4** I like pizza. ☐

5 I'm wearing a dress. ☐ **6** I've got a doll. ☐

7 I like chicken. ☐ **8** Look at my dog. It's big. ☐

9 It's sunny. ☐ **10** I'm wearing boots. ☐

19  **Read and write.**

boots   cold   ~~December~~   doesn't   hat   snowman

My favourite month is
1 <u>December</u>.
It's 2 _____ and snowy
in my country. I'm wearing a
coat and big 3 _____.
This 4 _____ is
mine. He's got a 5 _____!
My cat 6 _____ like
the snow.

20   **Draw your favourite month and write.**

My favourite month is

_____.

_____

_____

_____

_____

_____

Goodbye

1 Look and write.

~~castle~~   cave   clothes   dinner   doctor
farmer   mountain   shopping

1

2

3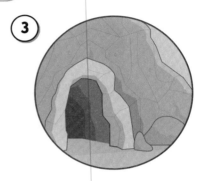

_____castle_____

_____

_____

4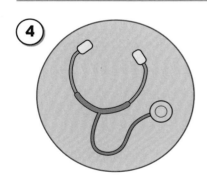

5

6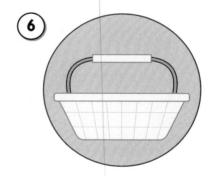

_____

7

8

_____

 **Read and draw.**

1 There's a photo on the TV.

2 There is a key in the door.

3 There are some shoes under the sofa.

4 There's a duck in the box.

5 There are some sunglasses next to the lamp.

6 There's an umbrella behind the bag.

 **Look at Activity 2. Read, circle and write.**

1 Where (is / (are)) the shoes? It's /(They're) <u>under the sofa</u>.

2 Where (is / are) the duck? It's / They're _____.

3 Where (is / are) the sunglasses? It's / They're _____.

4 Where (is / are) the photo? It's / They're _____.

4   **Listen and ✓ or ✗. Then write.**

Sally					
has got	✗	✓			
would like	✗				

Sally has got a _____ bike _____ and an _____ .

She hasn't got a _____, a _____ or a _____ .

She'd like a _____ and a _____. She wouldn't like a _____ .

5 **Complete for yourself. Then write.**

I've got					
I'd like					

I've got _____ .

I haven't got _____ .

I'd like _____ .

I wouldn't like _____ .

6 **Can you remember? Read and answer.**

1 What colour is Grandad's hair? <u>It's grey.</u>

2 Has Rose got curly hair? _____

3 How many cousins has Charlie got? _____

4 Is Charlie wearing a green T-shirt? _____

5 Has Ola got a big nose? _____

6 Is Uncle Dan a doctor? _____

7 Does Charlie like pizza? _____

8 Can Charlie do cartwheels? _____

a Yes, he does. **b** ~~It's grey.~~ **c** No, he isn't.

d No, she hasn't. **e** No, he can't. **f** Two.

g No, she hasn't. Her hair is straight. **h** No, it's blue and white.

7   **Write three questions for your friend to answer.**

1 _____? _____

2 _____? _____

3 _____? _____

Halloween

1  **Read and match.**

1 I'm a witch. I've got six sweets.

2 I'm a monster. I've got a pumpkin.

3 I'm a ghost. I've got four sweets.

4 I'm a pumpkin. I've got a bat.

a

b

c

d

e

f

g

h

2   **Read and circle.**

1 Do you like sweets?   Yes, I do. / No, I don't.

2 Do you like bats?   Yes, I do. / No, I don't.

3 Do you like pumpkins?   Yes, I do. / No, I don't.

4 Do you like Halloween?   Yes, I do. / No, I don't.

Christmas

1 **Look and write.**

| card | Christmas tree | present |
| sack | ~~Santa~~ | star | stocking |

① __Santa__   ② _____   ③ _____   ④ _____

⑤ _____   ⑥ _____   ⑦ _____

2 **Look and colour.**

1 = red   2 = green
3 = black   4 = blue
5 = yellow

1  **Read and match.**

1 Wake up, Easter Bunny!

2 Jump, Easter Bunny!

3 Turn around, Easter Bunny!

4 Fall down, Easter Bunny!

a

b

c

d

2 **Count and write.**

1 How many chicks? 5

2 How many flowers?

3 How many eggs?

4 How many rabbits?

Summer fun

1 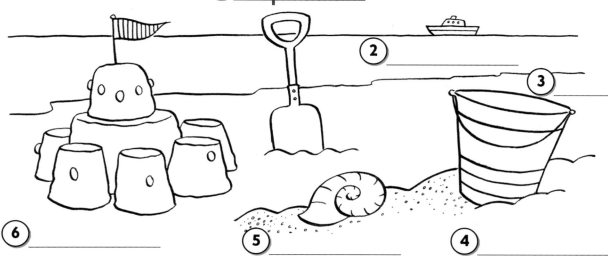 Look and write.

| bucket | sand | sandcastle | sea | shell | ~~spade~~ |

① spade

② _____

③ _____

④ _____

⑤ _____

⑥ _____

2 Sand art! Join the dots and write.

①

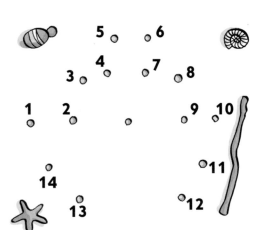

5 6
4 7 8
3
1 2 9 10

11

14
13 12

It's a _____.

②

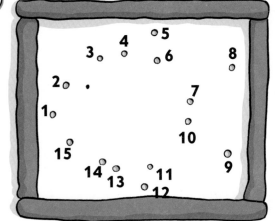

It's a _____.

Extra practice

1 ✏️ 🗣️ **Write the questions. Then say.**

1. name? your What's

   <u>What's your name?</u>

2. are How you?

   _____

3. your birthday? When's

   _____

4. today? day What it is

   _____

2 📖 ✏️ **Read and circle. Then write.**

1. What's ((this) / that) ?

   ((It's) / They're) a <u>teddy bear</u>.

2. What are (these / those)?

   (It's / They're) _____.

3. What's (this / that)?

   (It's / They're) a _____.

4. What are (these / those)?

   (It's / They're) _____.

How many cars are there? There are _____ cars.

How many boats are there? _____

 **Read and circle.**

1. Who's (**he** / she)? (**He's** / She's) my uncle.

2. Who are (they / there)? (They're / There) my cousins.

3. Where's my aunt? (He's / She's) (on / under) the sofa.

 **Read and circle.**

1. They're in the (living room / kitchen).

2. (There's / **There are**) two cousins.

3. The doll is (behind / on) the TV.

4. My uncle is next to my (aunt / cousin).

3

1 **Choose and write.**

can	can't	point	touch	~~wave~~	you

1 _____**Wave**_____ your arms.

2 _____ your fingers.

3 _____ your toes.

4 Oh, no! I _____ touch my toes.

5 Can _____ touch your toes?

6 Yes, I _____.

1   **Read and draw.**

I haven't got small eyes. I've got big eyes.

I've got a small nose and a small mouth.

I've got big ears. My hair is long and curly.

2 **Write *Yes, she has.* or *No, she hasn't.***

1 Has she got short hair?   No, she hasn't.

2 Has she got curly hair?   _____

3 Has she got small eyes?   _____

4 Has she got a small mouth?   _____

3  **Write correct sentences.**

1 She's got a big nose. She hasn't got a big nose. She's got a small nose.

2 She's got straight hair. _____

_____

3 She's got small ears. _____

_____

1 **Circle and write.**

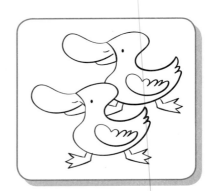

It isn't (big /(small)). It's (big / small).

(It's / They're) black.

It's got _____ legs.

(It's / They're) a _____ .

(It's / They're) small.

They aren't (black / white).

They're (black / white).

They've got _____ legs.

(It's / They're) _____ .

2 **Look at Activity 1. Read and match.**

1 Are the ducks brown?

2 Is the horse big?

3 Are the ducks small?

4 Is the horse grey?

a Yes, it is.

b No, it isn't.

c No, they aren't.

d Yes, they are.

1  **Read, look and circle.**

	✓	✓	✗	✓	✗	✗
	✗	✓	✓	✗	✓	✓

1 He ((likes) / doesn't like) fish.

2 She (likes / doesn't like) apples.

3 Does he like bananas? (Yes, he does. / No, he doesn't.)

4 Does she like chicken? (Yes, she does. / No, she doesn't.)

2 **Read and circle.**

1 There's ((some) / any) cheese.

2 There are (some / any) apples.

3 There isn't (some / any) milk.

4 There aren't (some / any) bananas.

3 **Look at Activity 2. Read and match.**

1 Is there any cheese?

2 Is there any pizza?

3 Are there any apples?

4 Are there any beans?

a No, there aren't.

b Yes, there is.

c Yes, there are.

d No, there isn't.

7

1 🖊️ **Choose and write.**

am	are	I'm	like	not	purple
	~~wearing~~		would		

1 Are you _____wearing_____ shoes and socks?

2 Yes, I _____.

3 _____ wearing blue shoes and pink socks.

4 _____ you wearing purple shoes?

5 No, I'm _____.

6 Would you _____ some purple shoes?

7 Yes, I _____. Thank you!

8 Now I'm wearing _____ shoes and pink socks!

1 **Choose and write.**

do	like	mine	that	they're	those

~~weather~~ windy

1 What's the __weather__ like?

2 It's _____.
Good!

3 Do you _____
windy days?

4 Yes, I _____.

5 What are
_____?

6 _____ kites.

7 This kite is _____
and _____ kite
is yours.

8 I like windy days!

Picture dictionary

Unit 1

Toys

| train | bike | ball | car | doll | boat | teddy bear | kite | lorry |

 Numbers

10	11	12	13	14	15
ten	eleven	twelve	thirteen	fourteen	fifteen

16	17	18	19	20	21
sixteen	seventeen	eighteen	nineteen	twenty	twenty-one

22	23	24	25	26	27
twenty-two	twenty-three	twenty-four	twenty-five	twenty-six	twenty-seven

28	29	30	40	50
twenty-eight	twenty-nine	thirty	forty	fifty

 Social Science

| bus | motorbike | lorry | plane | helicopter |

Unit 2

 ## My family

daughter   son

aunt   uncle

granny   grandad

cousins

 ## At home

house

flat

hall

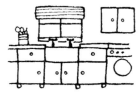

kitchen

living room

bedroom

bathroom

attic

 ## Social Science

baby

children

grandparents

young   parents   old

Unit 3

Body movements

 shake your body

 nod your head

 wave your arms

 point your fingers

touch your toes

 clap your hands

 stamp your feet

 move your legs

Actions

 swim

 climb

 catch a ball

 stand on your head

 throw a ball

 swing

 do cartwheels

 do the splits

P.E.

 pull

 push

 hop

 skip

Unit 4

My face

 hair   ears    eyes   nose    mouth

 Adjectives

 long   short   curly   straight

 dark   blond   neat   messy

 Maths

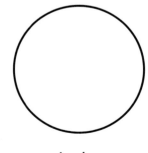 circle   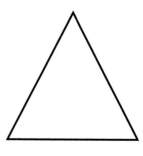 triangle   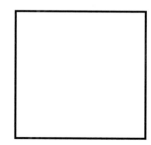 square    rectangle

Unit 5

Farm animals

 horse

 duck

 hen

 sheep

 cow

 goat

 turkey

Wild animals

 bat

 crow

 frog

 skunk

 owl

 lizard

 rat

 fox

Natural Science

 awake

 asleep

 night

 day

Unit 6
Food (1)

 rice

 bananas

 pizza

 burger

 fish

 chicken

 apples

 salad

 eggs

 ## Food (2)

 cereal

 grapes

 potatoes

 pancakes

 beans

 pineapple

 coconut

 pasta

 sweetcorn

 toast

 ## Natural Science

 cut

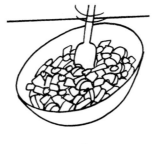 mix

 fry

 cook

Unit 7
Clothes (1)

 dress

 T-shirt

 socks

 skirt

 shoes

 trousers

 jacket

 hat

Clothes (2)

 pyjamas

 trainers

 shirt

 coat

 jeans

 helmet

 cap

 jumper

 glasses

 boots

Social Science

 nurse

 police officer

 firefighter

 chef

Unit 8

 ## Weather

windy	rainy	sunny	snowy	cloudy	stormy

 ## Activities

ride a bike	fly a kite	make a snowman	go for a walk

go to the beach	read a book	take a photo	watch TV

 ## Social Science

freezing	cold	warm	hot

Pearson Education Limited
Edinburgh Gate
Harlow
Essex CM20 2JE
England
and Associated Companies throughout the world.

Poptropica® English Islands

© Pearson Education Limited 2017

Editorial and project management by hyphen

First published 2017
Sixth impression 2019
ISBN: 978-1-2921-9823-1

Set in Fiendstar 17/21pt
Printed in Neografia, Slovakia

Acknowledgements: The publisher would like to thank Linnette Ansel
Erocak, Tessa Lochowski, Laura Miller and José Luis Morales, Steve
Elsworth, and Jim Rose for their contributions to this edition.

Illustrators: Chan Sui Fai, Adam Clay, Moreno Chiacchiera (Beehive
Illustration), Tom Heard (The Bright Agency), Andrew Hennessey, Marek
Jagucki, Sue King (Plum Pudding Illustration), Stephanine Lau, Katie
McDee, Bill McGuire (Shannon Associates), Jackie Stafford, Olimpia Wong
and Yam Wai Lun

Picture Credits: The publisher would like to thank the following for their
kind permission to reproduce their photographs:

(Key: b-bottom; c-centre; l-left; r-right; t-top)

123RF.com: 106 (nod), 108 (hen), 109 (pizza), 109 (rice), Jacek
Chabraszewski 106 (wave), Jose Manuel Gelpi Diaz 106 (point), David
Franklin 110 (hat), isselee 108 (goat), nrey 108 (duck); **Alamy Stock
Photo:** MIXA 106 (stamp feet); **Fotolia.com:** Robert Kneschke 35cr;
Pearson Education Ltd: Studio 8 104 (car), 106 (move legs), Trevor
Clifford 106 (clap), Rafal Trubisz 104 (doll), 106 (shake); **Shutterstock.
com:** Ilya Akinshin 104 (kite), AM-STUDiO 104 (teddy bear), Blend
Images 35r, Nikolay Dimitrov - ecobo 104 (train), Christopher Elwell 108
(turkey), hamurishi 104 (bike), Eric Isselee 108 (cow), 108 (horse), 108
(sheep), Karkas 110 (jacket), 110 (shoes), 110 (skirt), MShev 106 (touch
toes), Maks Narodenko 109 (apples), 109 (bananas), Nattika 109 (eggs),
Olga Nayashkova 109 (salad), Nitr 109 (burger), Richard Peterson 104
(ball), Olga Popova 110 (socks), pzAxe 110 (dress), sevenke 110 (T-shirt),
Roman Sigaev 110 (trousers), tetxu 109 (fish), Dani Vincek 109 (chicken),
Becky Wass 35l, wavebreakmedia 35cl, Mark Yuill 104 (boat)

Cover images: *Back:* **Fotolia.com:** frender r; **Shutterstock.com:** Denys
Prykhodov l

All other images © Pearson Education